FAMOUS ★

SURVIVAL WILDLIFE EXPERTS

Jonny Zucker

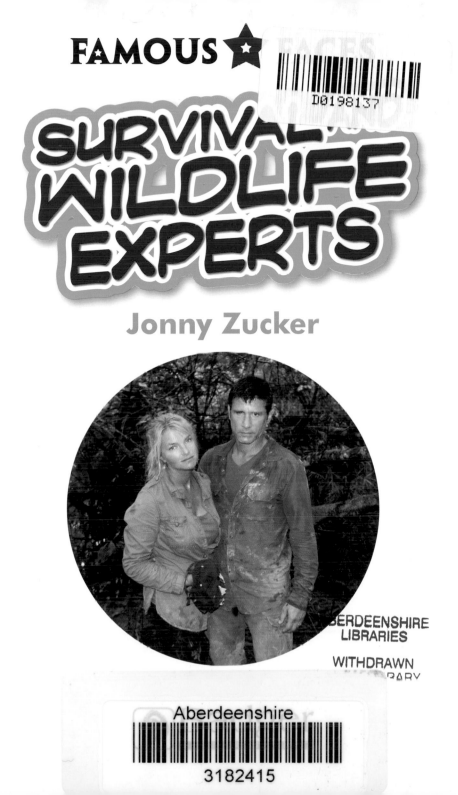

Badger Publishing Limited
Oldmeadow Road,
Hardwick Industrial Estate,
King's Lynn PE30 4JJ
Telephone: 01438 791 037

www.badgerlearning.co.uk

2 4 6 8 10 9 7 5 3 1

Survival and Wildlife Experts ISBN 978-1-78464-363-8

Text: © Jonny Zucker 2015
Complete work © Badger Publishing Limited 2015

Publisher: Susan Ross
Project editor: Paul Rockett
Senior editor: Danny Pearson
Editorial coordinator: Claire Morgan
Designer: Jason Billin / BDS Publishing Ltd

Picture credits: ArtStudioHouse/Shutterstock.com: 29; BBC Photo Library: 14; Bildagentur Zoonar GmbH/Shutterstock.com: 21; David Canterbury/www.selfrelianceoutfitters.com: 6; carrie-nelson/Shutterstock.com: 22; cyo bo/Shutterstock.com: 7bc; Czuber/Dreamstime. com: 10; Gallo Images/Alamy: 16; Deyan Georgiev/Shutterstock.com: 30; Mykel Hawke/ www.mykelhawke.com: 1, 27, 28; Gail Johnson/Shutterstock.com: 24; Lucky-photographer/ Shutterstock.com: 4,11; Susana Martins/Shutterstock.com: 15; Brittany Mason/Shutterstock.com: 26; Mercurio/Shutterstock.com: 7b; Roman Mikhailiuk/Shutterstock.com: 5; visa netpakdee/ Shutterstock.com: 17; Kellie Nightlinger/wildwomanoutdoors.com: cover, 8; Passakorn sakulphan/Shutterstock.com: 7tc; pelena/Shutterstock.com: 7t; s_bukley/Shutterstock.com: 25; John Sparks/naturepl: 18; Les Stroud Productions Inc./lesstroud.ca:12; Jack Sullivan/Alamy: 20; Vadym Zaitsev/Shutterstock.com: 13b; vnlit/Shutterstock.com: 9; Volga/Shutterstock.com: 13t; WENN Ltd/Alamy: 23; www.BillionPhotos.com/Shutterstock.com: 13c.

Attempts to contact all copyright holders have been made. If any omitted would care to contact Badger Learning, we will be happy to make appropriate arrangements.

FAMOUS ★ FACES

SURVIVAL AND WILDLIFE EXPERTS

Contents

Vocabulary

Do you know these words? Look them up in a dictionary and then see how they are used in the book.

anxiety

blizzards

cordage

dicing

forages

hostile

tinder

trophy hunters

For thousands of years human beings have faced floods and blizzards, snowstorms and baking desert heat.

To survive in these conditions we have had to learn how to find water, hunt for food, build shelters, make tools and work with animals.

The difference between learning these skills and not learning them is the difference between life and death.

CHAPTER 1:
LIVING OFF THE LAND

DAVID CANTERBURY ★

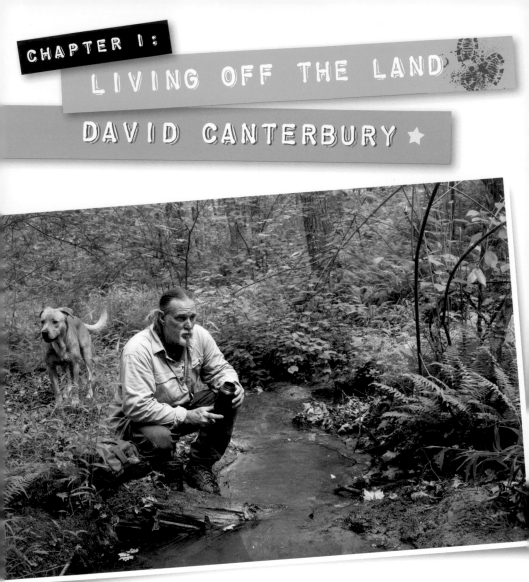

Survival expert David Canterbury doesn't just live off the land, he uses the land to make his own tools. There's nothing he can't make with stones, branches and leaves.

He has made knives, spoons, bowls, plates and even a kettle.

DAVID CANTERBURY'S FIVE Cs OF SURVIVABILITY

To survive in the desert Canterbury says you need ALL of the five Cs below:

★ **a cutting tool** – for chopping wood and hunting animals

★ **a combustion device** – something to light a fire such as flints or, to make things easier, matches!

★ **cover** – a tent, tarpaulin or self-made shelter

★ **a container** – anything to catch rainwater such as a flask or water bottle

★ **cordage** – a rope or similar tying device to help move between trees and over water

Kellie's father started teaching her how to hunt animals for food when she was three-years-old.

After many adventures Kellie focussed on exploring glaciers. She makes many of her own tools including harpoon guns. This comes in handy when she is attacked by animals.

TOP THREE DANGERS KELLIE HAS FACED:

1.
attacked by a swarm of bees

2.
set upon by an alligator

3.
crushed by a collapsing wall of ice

Cody Lundin knows how to survive in the wild.
He finds rainwater to drink and plants to eat.
He has travelled to some of the most remote places
on the planet.

FAMOUS GEAR ★★

Whatever the weather,
Lundin treks in shorts
and bare feet!

Lundin's home is high in the baking Arizona desert, where he lives 'off-the-grid' (without electricity).

He collects rainwater to drink, forages for food, and composts any waste products.

Lundin believes that humans can survive for 'some time' in pretty much any environment.

★★ FACT! ★★

When the *Jacson-4* boat sank off the coast of Nigeria in 2013, only the ship's chef Harrison Okene survived. He found a 4ft sq pocket of air in the boat and waited there until he was rescued. He survived in the air bubble for 62 hours, taking small sips of Coca-Cola, while sharks circled his location.

CHAPTER 2

GOING IT ALONE

LES STROUD ★

Les Stroud doesn't take camera crews on his treks. He likes to go it alone. In his TV show *Survivorman*, he went to some of the most hostile places on Earth and filmed it all by himself.

Stroud spent the first year of marriage living with his wife, Susan Jamison, in the Canadian wilderness. They built their own tipi and a shelter for the winter.

Tools they used for building shelters, chopping wood, cooking and washing included:

an axe

a hammer

a bow-saw

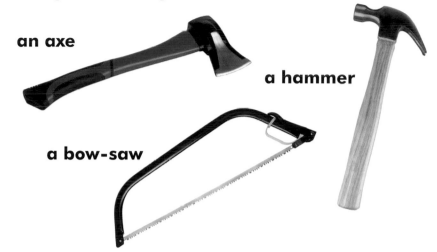

Stroud and Jamison eventually got divorced. Living under those conditions can lead to lots of arguments and anxiety!

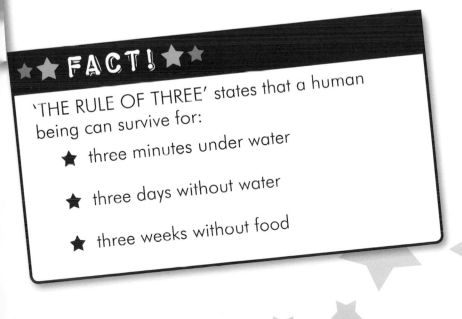

★★ FACT! ★★

'THE RULE OF THREE' states that a human being can survive for:

★ three minutes under water

★ three days without water

★ three weeks without food

HELEN SKELTON

In 2010, TV presenter Helen Skelton smashed the world record for the longest solo kayak journey.

She kayaked the entire 3,234.79km of the River Amazon as a challenge for *Sport Relief*.

Helen's kayak diary entry:

I was getting seasick and heat exhaustion and was covered with blisters and bites and boils.

As if kayaking wasn't enough, in 2012 Helen went on to become the first person to reach the South Pole by bicycle! She also used skis and a kite on the journey. On the specially made bike, she travelled 165.76km of the total 800km journey.

For the kite ski section of the journey she beat another world record: the fastest 100km by kite ski.

A kite ski works with strong winds pushing the kite forward, which in turns pulls the person along on skis.

CHAPTER 3:

MAKING WILD ANIMAL FRIENDS

KEVIN RICHARDSON ★

Thanks to his YouTube videos going viral, 'lion whisperer' Kevin Richardson is known all over the world.

Growing up in South Africa he saw how big cats, especially lions, were attacked and killed by trophy hunters. He wants to stop big cats becoming extinct, so he started working to protect lions, cheetahs and leopards.

Richardson now runs a special centre, called The Kingdom of the White Lion, in South Africa. Tourists are allowed to visit but they can't interact with the lions, hyenas and cheetahs there, as it takes years of practice to become a lion whisperer.

Richardson has been bitten and clawed many times. He says this is not due to the lions' aggression, but is the normal manner in which they 'play' with each other.

Kevin's diary entry

A lion is not a possession . . .
you must pay attention and develop
your bond just like with any relationship.

★★ FACT! ★★

A century ago there were over 100,000 tigers in the wild. Today there are around 3,200. If more is not done to save these majestic creatures they could be gone from our planet in mere decades.

David Attenborough is the most famous naturalist in the world.

As a child he collected fossils and newts.

He served in the British navy and went on to work for the BBC. In his TV series, *Life on Earth*, he became one of the first humans to sit among mountain gorillas.

Attenborough has made TV programmes about all kinds of animals, covering their whole lives from birth until death.

Attenborough says:

'*The future of life on earth depends on our ability to take action.*
Many people are doing what they can, but real success can only come if there's a change in our societies.'

★★ FACT! ★★

To make his *Life of Birds* TV series, Attenborough travelled over 411,992km.

★ CHRIS PACKHAM ★

As a presenter of TV programmes like *The Really Wild Show* and *Inside the Animal Mind,* Chris Packham has become a household name.

Chris is also an expert wildlife photographer and his photos have been exhibited all over the globe. He is particularly interested in kestrels and bats.

STOPPING THE BIRD KILLERS

In 2014, Chris spent days tracking hunters that were shooting and killing wild birds in Malta. Sometimes he only got four hours sleep a night, as the hunters like to shoot in darkness.

In the same year, Chris was named Conservation Hero of the Year.

The marsh harrier (above) is just one of the birds Chris has been trying to save from hunters in Malta.

THE DAILY NEWS

4 September 2006

DEATH IN THE WILD

The world has been shocked to hear of the death of 'Crocodile Hunter' Steve Irwin. Wildlife expert and conservationist, Irwin was stabbed in the chest by a stingray while filming underwater for a forthcoming TV series.

Irwin's daughter Bindi was only eight when Steve died, but she and her mother decided that she would continue her father's conservation and wildlife work.

Ray Mears was inspired by his school judo teacher, who had fought and survived behind enemy lines in World War Two.

Mears began tracking foxes on the North Downs in southern England, spending days following old trails. Unable to afford a tent, he started building shelters so he could camp out at night. He used all of his senses to study areas for traces of animals. This included looking for pawprints on the ground and tiny strands of fur caught in trees, as well as picking up smells to help track a whole range of animals.

★ TRACKING A KILLER ★

Mears placed himself in great danger in 2010 when he agreed to help the police. They wanted him to track down a killer who was hiding out in some woodland. With Mears' help the police found their man.

★ BEAR GRYLLS ★

Edward 'Bear' Grylls served in the Territorial Army
with the SAS. He has presented many television shows
including *Born Survivor*, *Mission Survive* and *The Island*.
He is also Britain's youngest-ever Chief Scout.

★ ALLIGATOR ALERT ★

In *Mission Survive*, Grylls knelt down beside a huge alligator and held its mouth closed while talking to celebrities about its awesome killing power!

★ MYKEL HAWKE ★

Mykel Hawke learned a lot of his survival skills as a captain in a US special forces unit. He has also worked as a bodyguard and private investigator.

Hawke spent some of his military service working as a medic, so he has detailed knowledge of how to deal with injuries when hospitals are hundreds of kilometres away.

Hawke rose to fame in TV shows. One of these, *Lost Survivors*, involved him and his wife Ruth England — another survival expert — being dropped into extremely remote locations.

With no maps or technology and very few supplies, they had to find food and water, and somehow get themselves to a safe location.

★★ FACT! ★★

Unless you can see that the source of a water supply is completely fresh (i.e. you catch or collect the water at the source yourself) then all water in the wild must be boiled before being drunk or serious diseases can be picked up.

CHAPTER 6

SURVIVAL TIPS

Survival kit

To survive in the wild and live off the land you will need:

- ★ **water**
- ★ **food**
- ★ **basic tools** (knife, hammer, saw)
- ★ **glucose tablets** (for energy)
- ★ **medical kit**
- ★ **comfortable walking shoes**
- ★ **change of clothing**
- ★ **rope**

What other items would you choose to take with you into the wild?

How to build the perfect campfire:

1 Dig a fire pit and surround it with stones.

2 Put some tinder (tiny twigs and sticks) in the centre.

3 Stack some kindling (larger pieces of wood) in a tipi (tent-like) structure.

4 Light the tinder in a few places.

5 As the fire takes, carefully add larger logs.

What makes Les Stroud stand out from the other 'TV' survivors? (page 12)

★ ★ ★ ★ ★ ★

What was it that killed Steve Irwin? (page 22)

★ ★ ★ ★ ★ ★

How did Ray Mears place himself in extra danger? (page 24)

★ ★ ★ ★ ★ ★

What dangerous creatures has Kellie Nightlinger faced? (page 9)

★ ★ ★ ★ ★ ★

What are the five Cs of surviving in the wild? (page 7)

★ ★ ★ ★ ★ ★

Why did Helen Skelton kayak the length of the River Amazon? (page 14)

★ ★ ★ ★ ★ ★